Emotions

Love, Feelings, Pain

Angela Herrick

AuthorHouse™
1663 Liberty Drive
Bloomington, IN 47403
www.authorhouse.com
Phone: 1-800-839-8640

© 2011, 2014 by Angela Herrick. All rights reserved.

No part of this book may be reproduced, stored in a retrieval system, or transmitted by any means without the written permission of the author.

Published by AuthorHouse   06/23/2015

ISBN: 978-1-4634-2298-1 (sc)
ISBN: 978-1-4634-2300-1 (hc)
ISBN: 978-1-4634-2297-4 (e)

Library of Congress Control Number: 2011915705

Print information available on the last page.

Any people depicted in stock imagery provided by Thinkstock are models, and such images are being used for illustrative purposes only.
Certain stock imagery © Thinkstock.

This book is printed on acid-free paper.

Because of the dynamic nature of the Internet, any web addresses or links contained in this book may have changed since publication and may no longer be valid. The views expressed in this work are solely those of the author and do not necessarily reflect the views of the publisher, and the publisher hereby disclaims any responsibility for them.

Contents

Introduction xi
Dedication xv

CHAPTER 1
PART I   LOVE

Love 3
My Inspiration Comes 4
Beauty 5
Love, You're So Sweet 8
Love Each Morning 9
Love, You Know the Lonely Hearts. 10
I Was Enjoying Spending Time with You, ... 11
I Fell in Love! with You 13
Life Has a Lot of Wonderful Things 14
I Fall in Love 15
I Am Happy Only with You 16
You Love to Give Presents and Gifts Away 17
Your Love Is Warm 18
You Need Support 20
I Told You, I Love You! 21
I Felt You from Our First Meeting 22
Could you come? 23
Hear My Heart 24
Staring at me, your eyes 26
I Imagine Your Touches 27
You Gave Me Feeling 28

I Think of You Always	29
You Ask Me about Love?	30
I Openly Talk about Feeling	31
You Never Could Imagine	32
I Will Always Love You	33
Darling, I Thought	34
I Can See You're in Love	35
I Love You More than Anyone	36
You Said, "I Love You!"	37
You promised	38
Without Love and Feeling	39
Love Always Needs an Ointment of Shine	40
I Want to Tell You Something	41
My Feelings Were Born	42
I Love You Very Much	43
You Gave Me Many Things	44
You Sent Me a Note with Sweet Words	45
Hope Comes from You	46
All Happiness and Joy in Us	47
I Love to Hear Your Soft Voice	48
You Were Thinking of Me	49
My Feeling, So Strong	50
I Learn to Read Your Eyes	51
You Left Me Alone	52
I Am with You on This Warm Night	53
You Have a Pain	54
Sweet Moments	56
You Have a Doubt	57
I Don't Believe	58
You Will Never Believe It	59
You Steal My Love	61
I Disappoint You	62

My Heart Is Broken..63
Two Women, Two Hearts..64
Love—stronger..65
A Real Woman...66

PART II   FEELINGS

Voices...73
The Best Feeling Is Joy..77
Emotions, They Come and Go...78
Regrets Always Press Us Down...79
Oh, How Emotionally...80
You Can Have a Million Friends..81
Everyone Has a Talent..82
I Love to Change the Time...83
How Sweetly You Play...84
Every Day Has a Name..85
The Age Has Levels...86
Life Never Turns Back...87
Wealth Is Deceitful...88
Nothing in the World..89
I Love a Silent Talk..90
Sometimes I Don't Know...91
You Are Happy for Things...92
When Will Stars Move...93
I Put My Trust in You...94
I Chose to Die..95
Patience, You Saved Me...96
No One Loves the Broken People..97
You Were My Best Friend..98
You Wanted to Tell Me Something..99
Time Is a Powerful Thing...100
The Human Beings...101

You Want to See Me...102

Please Don't Think of Me...103

Truth Is Pure..104

Flowers Are a Beautiful Creation 106

My Eyes Couldn't Close for Many Hours................................107

PART III   PAIN

TEARS..111

If You Have No Pain..115

My Soul Cries...116

Pain Is Not a Welcome Feeling...117

After Many Tears...118

How Blind I Was..119

The Beautiful Picture 120

Revenge...121

You think I don't know your fear?..123

We Never Understand Each Other 124

If I would ask you to come?..125

I Cry A Lot,...126

I cry, even my days was good,..127

You cry, I cry..128

You Know All My Pain 129

I Need Your Trust..130

I Try to Forget Everything 131

I Am Not Able to Forgive..132

I Saw You Cry..133

I Learn to Control My Emotions 134

I Have a Talent to Heal Others...135

My Inside Complaint...136

I Never Can Learn...137

The Pain Never Leaves My Heart...138

If I Could Start My Life Again 139
The Pain Pierced My Heart 140
Extremes 142
Life Never Comes Alone 143
We Came in This World 145
Life Is Time 146
Life Is a Gift of God. 147
My soul is in trouble when I see the needy and poor. 148

CHAPTER 2   WHAT IS LOVE?

Introduction 153
Dedicated 157
Where Lives My Love? 159
Two Stars 173
A MIRACLE CAN HAPPEN 192
Joy of Love 212

Introduction

The human nature, what God created,

A most beautiful creation of God's art.

God filled the human creature with human emotions:

Love, beauty, feelings, desires, and many emotions.

The all-sweet things from above, which mean

The all-good spirit from God.

The love. It is the best gift, the best sweet spirit from God, but

Love also produces many other emotions, such as pain,

Revenge, and many other desires.

What you have most is this air, the spirit of love,

That higher would your emotions be.

I repeat many times that I cannot live

Without a love—a/ sweet love/—

That comes from my sweetest Lord,

Whom I love unconditionally—and this spirit of love/

That God generously gave me.

A human being can express

Emotions in different ways, and it is true that

Everyone has different experiences.

Everyone has his or her own range of emotions,

Life experience, and just human affairs.

Emotion is air to live, air that fills our lungs and sustains our hearts.

Pain is also an emotion of hurts.

We human beings always love to have

All that is good, if not the best,

But pain may be for our own good.

Some heartache may be helpful for our experience of life,

Nevertheless, love is the reason to live.

Love is a sweet emotion. It deepens the soul and touches the heart.

Love shows her sweetness with touching kisses for loved ones.

Love is harmony of body and joyous, soul.

Love is an emotion that always wants

To hold a loved one with protective hugs.

Love is that has feeling and desire to reach out to a loved one.

— Emotions —

Love without kisses cannot survive.

It will be a cold and frozen love.

Love is a warm emotion that wants a whole body to feel it, feel you.

To feel your heart, your breast, your neck, your hair,

Your lips, your ears, and your eyes,

Not only in one place, but in all.

Love is a feeling, not an exercise that soon will tire and bore you.

Love lives in the heart forever and is

Never enough for only one if it is real.

A forever love, born in a heart on Earth, will live in heaven.

Nothing can judge everything. This is my own truth,

My own experience of this life,

My own emotion of human feeling,

My own life led by God, always.

Dedication

To my beloved savior and

Precious redeemer.

Vera Bergh.

You gave me life.

I live because of you.

I had tolerated pain,

But you healed it.

When I cried, you wiped my tears.

When I was disappointed and despairing,

When I was angry and weak,

You healed me inside.

You lifted me up.

I live because of you.

My life is you.

I cannot better describe

— *Angela Herrick* —

How you are all my life,

How I love more than anything,

How I live because of you.

You have done so much for me.

You were always near.

Without you, I wouldn't

Be able to do anything.

You were my shoulder,

A part of my life!

In my heart forever, it will be only you.

I will always remember

That I live because of you!

Part I

Love

Love is never half,

Love is always everything.

Love

Love is an emotion of the heart.

Beauty is an emotion of the eyes.

Wisdom is an emotion of the mind.

Passion is an emotion of desires.

My Inspiration Comes

My inspiration comes from

A bright sun on a beautiful morning.

My inspiration comes from

A precious nature which provides a green tree and singing birds.

My inspiration comes from

Earthly beauty that God created with unison.

Beauty

Beauty is high emotion before our eyes.

An object is beautiful because you see it with eyes of beauty.

You may see it as clearly beautiful; you cannot see its reality.

Beauty is an emotion that makes reality much better, much finer.

Beauty loves everything about you.

In the eye of the emotion of beauty,

Everything is much more wonderful,

Much sweeter.

The beauty of any action you will come to love as One.

You will come to love not only the person, but also how that person

Uses the emotion of beauty—

How she sits /beautifully/, how she eats beautifully,

Or how she walks beautifully.

Who you love might be the beauty of your world.

You will love the whole of the beautiful person,

The all of the beautiful spirit.

The beautiful spirit can only inhabit a good person.

Beauty in one/whole body/ is what God created and filled with a sweet spirit.

God created these jewels,

This great and precious art. All in one.

You will desire not some part of it, but everything.

Beauty is a sweet emotion given to each one of us as gift.

Some may have more sparkles, some may have less,

But all of us have this jewel of God's art.

We have to love everything that we receive.

All beauty is work from above that was made for each one of us.

Take good care of the precious things,

The jewels love to shine, always.

The jewel always has a price, and it can always be repaired,

But never should you disappear it.

Everyone is an individual stone; we are all jewels.

We are all precious in different ways.

No one can compare the works of God,

We are all incomparable. Jewels.

Emotions

As with all precious stones, some are rated level one, some are rated level ten,

More or less, some are never rated.

Beauty is a visible stone, let it count so others can see God's art.

Let God be happy for what He has done. Let God have the joy,

And never lose what was made by God.

Let your beauty shine away, and take care that it should look clean,

Pure, and always lovely.

Open your eyes to see it. Good eyes will see it well,

Precious eyes will see precious things.

Beauty in the world cannot be missed by God above.

It is a natural gift, which nature can always restore.

Beauty has a presence at any age, as nature has

Her four seasons and all of them are lovely.

Beauty is beautiful people, who love God, who enjoy God's art.

Beauty comes from above, and we are blessed to have it!

Love, You're So Sweet

Love, you're so sweet.

Love, you have a power over our hearts.

Love, you're a honey spirit from above.

Love, you can melt any iceberg, any rock.

Is this is real love?

Love, you're the reason to live.

Love, you're oxygen for the heart.

Love is never enough for lovers.

Is this is real love?

Love, you're the harmony of all desires.

Love, you're the comfort for all discomforts.

Love, you're the key to all miracles.

This is real love.

Love Each Morning

Love each morning,

Each afternoon and evening.

Love at sunrise and sunset.

Love to all birds and all trees,

To the blue sky and her moon and stars.

Love to the mountains and creeks.

Love to the streams, rivers, seas, and oceans.

Love to gardens and flowers.

Love to all the seasons and their beauty.

Love to wild animals and our pets.

Love all people who care for you.

Love, love, love forever the Lord.

Love your God!

Love, You Know the Lonely Hearts.

Love, you know the lonely hearts.
For someone, you gave everything.
For another, you gave nothing.
Love, your balance is not fair!
All people deserve you!

Who am I to tell love
Who should be loved most?
Love knows all our hearts, and decides
What would be best.

Love searched for the place where
She will be at last /and live forever/.
Love always wants the best!

Love searched our hearts and tested.
Love, please make sure you search mine
And let no one else break it.
Let no one steal or corrupt it.
One love, no one else.

I Was Enjoying Spending Time with You,

I was enjoying spending time with you.

I was enjoying listening to you.

My soul had a rest; your soul did, too.

I was watching you for long time.

Would that I could have been with you for longer.

If you could know how to love a woman,

You would know joy.

If you could know how to kiss a woman,

I would have stayed longer with you.

If only you could know how to touch a woman,

How to hug, how to love

A woman.

— Angela Herrick —

Without love, I listened to you,

Watched you, and spent my time with you.

I let my soul find someone else

Who knows all the sweetness and joy of love!

Love must fill the two halves of our passion.

It must bring joy to the soul and joy to the heart.

Tickle with treats of kisses and treats of hugs.

Then it will be perfect joy,

Joy of love!

I Fell in Love! with You

I fell in love! with you,

Not with your accumulations.

I fell in love!—

I saw kindness in your heart.

Please give everything away.

Please make others happy.

Me? I don't need anything.

I need only you.

And you will see that

Our love is—and will be—

Perfect!

Life Has a Lot of Wonderful Things

Life has a lot of wonderful things

And offers an abundance of bliss.

Choose what delights you..

Be the happiest person

In the world, not the richest!

I Fall in Love

I fall in love.

Deeply.

Everyday, I want to see you.

Everyday, all my thinking is of you.

Every night, I want to feel you.

Why give so much power to you?

Now, I'm not free.

I cannot

Live without you.

Can you imagine?

What would happen if

You were to leave me?

I cannot.

I Am Happy Only with You

I am happy only with you.

I don't know why, do you?

I always want to smile.

I don't know why, do you?

My inner being has joy.

My soul has peace.

I know why, do you?

I love you!

You Love to Give Presents and Gifts Away

You love to give presents and gifts away.

You love the surprises,

The fun, and the parties.

You love to ask questions.

I know what question

You have for me.

What do you like to receive?

Darling! I wish you could have this gift.

I wish as much that I might receive it, but I know you.

You are able to gave many gifts to the world,

Except what I desire most.

You not able to give what I need.

I need only love, the priceless gift!

Your Love Is Warm

Your love is warm.

Your love makes me feel you deeply.

I never can wait for your kisses.

I never can wait for your touches.

All sweet moments, all sweet feelings,

Just melt my heart.

Let our love be sweetest,

Our nights warmest and truest,

And our happiness longest.

Only your love gave me a desire to live.

All sweet moments, all sweet feelings,

Just melt my heart.

I never can wait for our nights to expose our love.

Kiss me; please kiss me as you always do.

Touch me gently and sweetly.

— Emotions —

I have never loved anyone like you.

You are the most precious being to me.

How could I have known

I would have a love

Who would know how to melt my heart?

You Need Support

You need support; you have made up your mind.

Your warm personality has you thinking you are the one.

You don't know how much I care for you,

Wish happiness for You, and desire to see you smile.

And your heart radiates, as does mine.

I advise you to taste all

The sweetness of love,

The bitterness of pain,

And the ups and downs of married life.

Then, compare it all and know that

The joy will come after the tears,

The lessons will come after the disappointments,

And nothing will be vain after all of this.

You will learn to live life emotionally

And deep.

I Told You, I Love You!

I told you, "I love you."

I told you, "You are my life."

A naive girl, I sacrificed everything for you,

And I chose wrongly for me.

Was I living in a dream?

Was it your coldness and old age

Which kept you from believing a girl

Who said she loved you?

Your closed mind never believed it.

Your frigid heart never accepted it.

One day, the girl who told you she loved you

Will be famous, and you will see.

You will come to the girl

To say,

"You once loved me."

I Felt You from Our First Meeting

I felt you from our first meeting,

As if we had many meetings before,

As if I had known you all my life.

I feel you as if you've been my loved one, always.

You fill me with sweet feelings and sweet thoughts.

You have power over me.

I don't even know where we are now?

Life only produces this passion once,

Creating a root for the tree of love.

I am powerless,

Please, stay with me now.

Forever!

Could you come?

Could you come?

I am very alone,

Very much alone.

I want you to come.

I wish I could be patient,

Wish I could wait. But

You have to know, without you,

My days are empty eternities.

I wish I could have you in all my days and nights,

And in my life always.

Please come and never leave.

Make a moment into a forever that

Will stay—you and me!

Hear My Heart

Hear my heart.

Listen to my voice.

Feel my sigh, my breath.

Take in my shaking body.

I am so very nervous,

You cannot imagine

How nervous I am.

The first time I touched you,

My body shook.

I trembled /inside/ my feeling was so strong.

All emotions arose to show

My desire. /I was very nervous/.

Please hold my body.

Please stop the trembling.

— Emotions —

I feel the warmth, and I will

Respond to the sweetness of love.

I have a desire to feel all of you,

To hold your body.

I don't want to miss a single touch.

I desire you,

You cannot imagine how much.

No one in the world desires you as I do.

I'm under the power of love!

Staring at me, your eyes

Staring at me, your eyes.

Show happiness.

I never knew your eyes chose me.

I never knew your eyes would lead me to this place.

Your eyes want my lips.

Your eyes reveal the power

Passion has over you!

I Imagine Your Touches

I imagine your touches and I tremble inside.

I imagine your kisses and my head swells, intoxicated by the thought.

If I let my imagination go deeper,

It would make me very weak.

I ask you to hold me, always tethered,

With your lovely hands and

The support of your precious breast,

So that I do not to fall to the ground.

You keep me up with your

Heart and mind.

I am in love with you!

I love you more than anyone /on Earth/.

You Gave Me Feeling

You gave me feeling and
I feel the joy come to me.

I think the world has nothing
As pretty, as beautiful, as you.
When I see your loving eyes
I don't question anything.
Your eyes speak to me,
And give me joy, give me you.

Your eyes tell me about your feelings and
Help me to be close to you, to be with you,
To feel their loving gleams.
Don't say anything, your eyes tell me all.

Never will I find such twinkling eyes
In this whole world because I love you!

I Think of You Always

I think of you always.

Always is now.

Is this strange?

You refuse me, but I gave you my heart.

No one can replace my heart.

Forgive me, forgive me.

My mind keeps jumping to you and my

Heart cannot leave you.

But you love someone else.

Time will be our judge.

I wish you a happy heart!

Forgive me, forgive me.

My mind keeps jumping to you and

My heart never will leave you,

Even though you refused me.

You Ask Me about Love?

You ask me about love?

You want to know,

How does love come?

You try to use sweet words,

You try to touch me.

I listen to your Heart.

Is there a place for love?

Is there a place for feeling?

Darling, don't try anything!

You have a most beautiful heart.

Love will desire to live in it.

This feeling comes from above!

I Openly Talk about Feeling

I openly talk about feeling,

Feeling deep emotions,

Which God is creating.

Love is the highest,

Sweetest emotion.

It is a gift of God!

I openly talk about love.

I cannot live without it, /Love/.

What my heart desires most

Is sometimes too high, I know.

But God is the only measure of such levels.

You Never Could Imagine

You never could imagine

How deeply I wanted you!

You never could imagine

How deeply I felt for you!

You never could imagine

How happy you made me!

Could you have imagined

What love can do?

I Will Always Love You

I will always love you

No matter what.

I will always think of you

Because, against your will,

My heart was broken!

Darling, I Thought

Darling, I thought

I knew what love was.

But, I never knew until now.

I think about you.

I'm crazy about you.

I only need your love, and

I ask only for your kisses and hugs.

I Can See You're in Love

I can see you're in love.

I know your thoughts, and I recognize your feelings,

You're in love.

I wish I felt the same.

I wish I could love you.

But my heart doesn't feel anything.

My pain keeps my heart closed.

I not able to love.

You see, we both have pain.

Your pain—leaving me.

My pain—leaving love..

We both have pain,

In love or not,

And we both need time to heal.

I Love You More than Anyone

I love you more than anyone.

I adore you more than anything.

I enjoy being with you.

How do you know I'm the one?

I feel you; I feel your heart.

I feel you in my presence.

I feel your soul; I feel your Love!

You Said, I Love You!

You said, "I love you!"

Yet, you kept no promises.

You said, "I love you!"

But you don't know the meaning.

You said, "I love you!"

You lied to me with beautiful words

That signified nothing to you.

You promised

You promised

To love me like no one else.

You promised

Only to make me happy.

You promised

Your kisses would be warmer than those of others.

You promised

To touch me only so sweetly.

But you forgot about only me.

Your love was passion.

Your love was fire.

I never reminded you about your promises to me.

I believed your kisses, your warm touches.

I believed your promises, but

You promised

These same things to others, not only to me?

Without Love and Feeling

Without love and feeling,

The life is not the life I wanted.

Without love there never will be happiness.

Without feeling there never will be love,

The one thing we need for life.

Feeling in your heart / love/,

Nothing else is better—

To fill your heart with feeling,

To be in love!

Love Always Needs an Ointment of Shine

Love always needs an ointment of shine.

Love always needs a fragrance of sweetness.

Love always needs a soft, beautiful word.

Love always needs a warm interior.

Love is a fire that needs wood to keep burning.

Love needs the fullness of feeling

That never puts out the blaze / inside /.

I Want to Tell You Something.

I want to tell you something;

I cannot to heal my pain.

I just want to see you.

I need to see your eyes,

Maybe this will help heal me.

Maybe I will see your regret,

Maybe you will find words of healing.

Your eyes—cold—as they always were.

I only dreamed of seeing a miracle, but

Your heart never melted.

My Feelings Were Born

My feelings were born of your heart.

I desired you not for a few nights.

I desired you for the rest of my life.

I have feelings, but look how painful they are.

Your heart bore nothing!

I Love You Very Much

I love you very much.

But you did not believe it, and

You put me to a difficult test,

Trial and suffering.

I sacrificed everything for you.

Now, you believe that

I love you very deeply!

You Gave Me Many Things

You gave me many things.

You gave me my desire.

You cared for me always, and

You were by my side.

I will always love

Everything and anything

About you!

You will be in my heart forever.

You Sent Me a Note with Sweet Words

You sent me a note with sweet words.

You sent me a note with lovely wishes.

You attended to my loneliness.

You showed me your wonderful personality.

You always will be blessed!

Hope Comes from You

Hope comes from you.

Faith, I will always hold and love you

Forever.

You're mine, hope, faith, and love.

It is always you!

All Happiness and Joy in Us

All happiness and joy in us,

All sweet moments and sweet feelings in us,

All good work and good intentions in us,

Only serve to open our good hearts!

I Love to Hear Your Soft Voice

I love to hear your soft voice, your beautiful words.

I love your sweet touches, your lovely kisses.

Have I ever told you?

Every sweet emotion stirs me inside.

You're so warm, my heart melts.

Darling, you should know that

You're the sweetest man in the world.

You Were Thinking of Me

You were thinking of me.

I was with you in your thoughts.

You sacrificed your time,

You opened your feeling.

Darling, everything else will pass away.

But sweet thoughts and sweet feelings

Will stay with you always!

My Feeling, So Strong

My feeling, so strong,

My passion, so deep,

I give them power.

With them, I can choose anyone,

No matter who.

I can go any place, but

I never will.

I'm crazy about only you!

I Learn to Read Your Eyes

I learn to read your eyes,

To know what your eyes can tell.

You open wide for me, and I can see everything.

Suddenly, your eyes change.

I am not able to read them; I cannot tell anything.

There is nothing left from the previous look.

You're not the same.

Your eyes are never clear,

And I cannot tell anything.

Your eyes, they're different,

Your eyes, they deceive now.

I / wish / to know why

You destroyed everything so fast.

You betrayed yourself.

I know because your eyes lie.

You betrayed me.

I know because you tried to hide it.

You Left Me Alone

You left me alone; a new lover appeared.

Times have changed; your life is a dream.

You impatiently pushed everything.

I just hope this will work, your dream,

But probably not.

How soon will it happen? How soon will it end?

I don't believe in fantasy, in sparkles in the air.

This rejection must be borne much higher!

I Am with You on This Warm Night

I am with you on this warm night.
I feel so joyful to see you smile.
I want to remember every moment.

I won't forget the white roses,
The gorgeous, sweet white roses,
I will always remember them as the ,
Bouquet of our love.

You gave me a gift, a brilliant evening,
Breezy and warm, like your
Radiant smile. But
White roses I will never forget.

Such sweet white roses—
Cheers for many years of happy love!
And a table set with white roses,
The bouquet of our love,
That I will remember always!

You Have a Pain

You have a pain, a broken heart.

Tenderly, I want to heal you.

I want embrace you in my love,

A medicine for all pain.

No, you are not ready.

You are not strong enough

For a new relationship.

I'm afraid you will miss

What may never come again, my love.

Don't wait; I cannot bear to see you suffer.

You cry, and I cry with you.

Your pain mirrors my pain.

No, you are not ready.

You are not strong enough for a new relationship.

Emotions

Let me heal you with my love.

There is nothing in the world I need—

Only to heal your sweet heart and

Give to you a new spirit of joy,

A new spirit of love.

Don't miss what never

Comes again, love.

No, you are not ready, not strong enough

For a new relationship, for a new love!

Sweet Moments

Sweet moments, sweet love,
I have these with you. I could feel
That the whole world is sweet because
You fill all the air in my universe. Only
With you am I always lifted up.

Sweet moments, sweet love,
I have these with you.
Love me, like no one else on Earth,
Love me like all in one.
I will tell all universes that
Your love is deep and sweet
My emotions go on, my love is real.

Sweet moments, sweet love,
I have these with you.
Love me like no one else
On Earth ever can.
You and I,
We are a sweet paradise!

You Have a Doubt

You have a doubt; you do not believe it.

In my opinion, you do not believe it.

Show me what makes you secure.

I will prove that I cannot

Live without you.

My love is so strong, my love is so real,

There's no reason not to believe it.

Out of doubt, out.

I love you—believe me—

More than anyone else in the world!

My love is so deep, so strong,

So real, you will believe it!

I Don't Believe

I don't believe that you have love.

I don't believe the love in your heart.

I can see you because I can see your eyes.

Please don't lie.

Your emotions are in the air; you cannot hide them.

I see you don't understand. In that way,

You are alone at heart.

Please let us acknowledge the truth.

Yes, I'm very lonely

When you answer, love.

Love, I ask you to come,

Come with a sweet heart.

I truly want to feel you in my heart.

When you come, I will never let you go.

I will never let you leave me!

You Will Never Believe It

You will never believe it,
My Love is very special.

You will never believe it,
My heart melts only for you.

You will never believe it,
I cannot forget you.

I have my own family now,
And I know you do, too.
We seem all happy, all smiles.

But you will never believe it,
I still love you!
What am I to do?

— Angela Herrick —

Two families seem so happy,
But what can I do?
I love you!

You will never believe
That my love is special,
But I will always love you!

You Steal My Love

You steal my love,

Which never belonged to you.

You steal my heart,

Which is not your possession.

I cannot lie this long.

Please understand that

I cannot to lie to my heart.

The heart always knows the truth.

I Disappoint You

I disappoint you.

My heart from pain pierced,

"Sorry!" never would be my excuse,

Only love would be my explanation.

I believe in love, and you believe in me.

Nothing will make a change.

If you can hold your pain,

I will suffer also.

I believe in Love, and you believe in me.

I will always love you,

Wish it or not!

My Heart Is Broken

My heart is broken.

Orchestra plays the hardest hits—

Something should take my pain away—

Orchestra, it could be you!

Play Beethoven for me / Symphony Number 5/.

My heart is broken. Please orchestra play and never stop.

I try never to think about it.

But inside I have pain;

My love was twice refused.

Why I fall in love?

Orchestra, play Tchaikovsky/ Symphony Number 3/.

That should take my pain away,

Orchestra, it could be you.

Play all the masterpieces,

Relieve my pain.

The hardest hits are in my heart right now.

Two Women, Two Hearts.

Two women, two hearts,

Found love and a harmony of souls,

A paradise on Earth.

Why should someone appear

Or behave as a man?

Never should a love of hearts

Change the natural state.

Love should be real!

Love—stronger

Love—stronger than any emotions,

Greater than any circumstances.

Love is our strength, our protection, our armed defense.

No one will ever be able to destroy or conquer it.

Love defeats everything!

A Real Woman

I don't know exactly the number of women

In this world.

But the world has more women than men.

All of humankind is important, but

While man may be the hands and shoulders,

Women are the face of the world.

A woman is beautiful and special

If she is willing to love herself,

If she is willing to remain true to her womanhood.

The real woman, who is feminine and sweet,

Knows that she came into this world

To emotionally support the men,

And be the everything for the children.

She is balm for the wounds,

And a shepherd of the soul.

The real woman, who loves herself,
Knows that any man
Will love a caring woman, too.
The real woman will have a real man
Who will provide and care for her.
A real woman never should have to work.

The real man will love his woman and
Will support her.
The real woman will love herself and
Know that the husband should go to work.

The real woman came into this world to be a woman.
The man came in this world to be a real man.

If the man loves his woman, he will work.
Women are the heart of love.
Without women it wouldn't be a real romance,
And a man without a woman won't be a real man.

The real woman is an expression of beauty and love.
The real woman should be sweet,
Respectfully and nicely treated.
She loves and respects herself.

The man will take care of this woman, the man will work,

To show his care and his love to his woman.

This is a real woman,

Who takes coffee to bed for her man's hands,

Who takes flowers from her man.

She never writes checks because that is the

Business of her husband.

She never drives a car, and she always wears heels.

She is a real woman!

Her wardrobe is full of beautiful things

Given to her from her loving man.

She has many gift boxes and each one she remembers

Because they are from him.

She waits for her man to come home from work.

She opens the door, and each time she has a new robe.

Each time her man has a smile.

They always have a reason to be happy,

To have a good time, relax, and

Always think about each other's feelings.

They never forget about love.

— *Emotions* —

The men are always physically stronger.
He will carry his woman,
Who loves to make everyone happy,
To the bed.

She is the woman; she came into this world
To show her love and respect.
She wants to be a real woman,
She wants love and anyone can see /her love/.

Anyone can be special, if he or she wishes it,
Any woman can be a real woman and understand that
A man should care for a woman and that
It is better for a man to work.

But love first comes from a real woman.
The real woman has emotions of love and joy.
A real woman has her special man,
And a real man has his special woman. Then
Life will be happiness and joy!
Nothing is better .

Part II

♥

Feelings come from the heart.

Voices

Our planet includes many sounds and voices.

Seven billon people on the planet means there are seven billon voices, too.

All of them are different and have different powers.

Never will you find the two same voices in the whole world.

Among all these voices, one voice moved me inside.

Soft and deep, among these billon voices, this one voice

Made me wonder *Why only this voice, not any other voice?*

Voices have power; even one voice has power

Over words, songs, voices, and hearts.

One voice can move your feelings, / move you to fall in love/.

Other voices may inspire your compassion.

And others may even spark your humility.

Soft or deep, amidst all of the ambient sound, no two are ever the same.

All voices have different sounds—they were formed

By our expressions and our emotions. /Feeling/.

The voices, as emotions, can change, like musical tunes of music,

But your voice will be always yours.

Your voice tells us about your inner feelings

And your emotions, too.

I wonder *why is it that one soft voice moves me inside? Only one?*

Why does this voice have a power over me?

It made me nervous, this one voice so powerful.

For a long time, I could not get over that sound

Which woke me up, like opera /music/ might.

I tried to find the answer to the burning question:

Why only this voice and none other?

Other voices I hear for a short time, then they are forgotten,

But this soft voice always deeply touched

Me; always went straight to the core.

I wonder, *What special powers does this voice have?*

Comparing all sounds, listening to many operas,

Symphonies, concerts, jazz ensembles, and pop music recordings,

— *Emotions* —

Always for a few hours, but

The music stops and the sounds have lasting no power over me.

One person has a voice that stays.

A soft sound, I cannot forget it.

It traps me in a trembling anxiety

Impossible for one voice in the whole world

To have this power over me!

Right?

I start another search, asking, *What voices can be found in nature?*

Who is the creator of the people's voices?

I am relieved when I find the answer: the one precious Creator

That over everything can be beautiful and precious,

Sweet and accessible,

That can to move us like no other.

She is greater than anything in the world,

She is our special feeling; she is our grace.

In the whole world, all humans have voices,

Soft or deep,

Sweet or mild.

The precious One, her art she never shares with anyone.

She has her own emotional way, the way of beauty and

The way of her impressive art.

She is the One—the precious Venus.

Venus, above all others on the planet, makes beautiful sounds,

And moves our emotions in different ways.

But one voice, your voice,

Is your special sound, your special natural art!

The Best Feeling Is Joy.

The best feeling is joy.

When you have love/ and no pain/,

When you appreciate all the days of your life,

When you are happy help to others,

When you easily forget the bad

(And remember the good)

When all your dreams come true,

When you find fairness,

When you laugh at a bird's conversation,

When your face smiles from the sun's /beams/,

When you're in harmony with your emotional world,

You are blessed.

No one can take joy, priceless joy, from you.

The great virtue is

To live simply but enjoy richly!

Emotions, They Come and Go

Emotions, they come and go.

Please let negative emotions go first,

I will try to hold the others.

The sweet ones, I never let go,

The love ones, I never let die.

No one can take these from me,

Secured in my heart,

Tethered by delight and joy,

What I have from my God!

Regrets Always Press Us Down

Regrets always press us down,

And push us to say, "Sorry."

Regrets make us sad,

Show our wrongs,

Our mistakes, and our misdeeds.

Regrets have depressive power.

And regrets have the power to teach.

Better never to do what you may regret!

Better never to put your trust in anything

You might regret.

I regret that I know Regret!

Oh, How Emotionally

Oh, how emotionally you tried to move me!

You called for jealousy

To help make me long for you.

You tried to keep company with others

To let the jealousy rule.

Believe that it hurt, but you are not the winner.

Jealousy will not help you; it will destroy you..

Jealousy is no friend of love; it allies with hate.

I will never use this danger key for love.

Where there is jealousy, there is no trust.

You Can Have a Million Friends

You can have a million friends.

But understand that

You need only one,

Who instantly might feel like millions.

Everyone Has a Talent

Everyone has a talent.

Everyone has a personality.

Everyone has a life.

Everyone is an individual.

The most beautiful talent is

To recognize and respect the hearts of others!

I Love to Change the Time

I love to change the time.

I love the best times to return to me.

I want all my years back

That I shared with you!

How Sweetly You Play

How sweetly you play.

How lusty you look.

How seductively your voice

And body makes moves.

Don't play. You don't have to.

No one has your touching voice.

No one has your lovely personality.

No one has your most beautiful heart.

No one has your sweet, natural gift.

You don't have to play!

Don't destroy the emotion of love.

This may never come again.

You may move another way, but

Please don't play.

I see your beauty; it needs

No seduction.

Every Day Has a Name

Every day has a name.

Every day makes our lives longer, but

Sometimes the everyday is the same.

And life seems stay in one place,

And go nowhere.

Nothing changes.

I don't know the name of the day.

I don't know if this is the day before; they are all the same.

Only, I know—same or not—each day makes us older!

The Age Has Levels

The age has levels.

The age has experiences.

The age has powers.

The age has a lovely feeling, but

Would it be enough to age,

And make the best of what was missed?

Life Never Turns Back.

Life never turns back.

Life never stops for anything.

Life keeps the beat to her own time.

For one person, life brings success.

For someone else, life brings failure.

Life, for all of us, brings a unique destiny.

Wealth Is Deceitful

Wealth is deceitful.

It allows more material things,

While taking away spiritual things.

More work—reduced time.

More worry—less joy.

More friends—fewer lovers.

More parties—less sleep.

More tension—impaired health.

Better to have less wealth—more happiness!

Nothing in the World

Nothing in the world is forever,

Only the words of God.

Nothing lives in our hearts forever,

Only Love.

One thing what lives forever,

In all of these / things /,

That we all have,

Is the soul!

I Love a Silent Talk

I love a silent talk.

I love to feel you without touch,

I love to smile while I see you in my mind's eye.

I love your peace and joy,

Your feeling of soul,

I am in soul's love!

Sometimes I Don't Know

Sometimes I don't know what time is.

Sometimes I don't know what day or year it is.

Sometimes I don't know where I am.

I believe, with my eyes wide open, but I do not see it.

My feet are walking, but I do not feel it.

I have no control; all control is high above me.

You Are Happy for Things.

You are happy for things when you have them.

You are happy for time when you have it.

You are happy for meetings when you have them.

You are happy for good looks when you have them.

But you are never happy for what you feel inside.

When Will Stars Move

When will stars move in my direction

And will the sun shine?

When will heavenly bliss rejoice

And make my life sing?

When will my heart be merry?

When will my eyes sparkle?

If I could be God,

I would know about His mystery!

I Put My Trust in You

I put my trust in you.

I believed in your promises.

I was faithful; I never counted my losses.

I sacrificed everything, always, for you.

You left me broke.

You left the sharks to tear me up?

Is this a reward for my loyal love?

How I can believe you? How?

I gave my life to you, not to the sharks.

But you won't take me and keep me

For a long time in a shark's mouth.

My life is dead, but no one

Will eat and no one will swallow.

Caught in the balance—not dead, not alive.

Are there worse things than being between out and in?

That is how I see my reward for my loyal love.

Please, show your power!

I Chose to Die

I chose to die—love, hold me!

I chose to give up—patience, keep me!

Everything broke apart, but

Love and patience overcame.

Love never lets you die.

Patience never lets you give up.

Hold these very tight—two powerful things.

In your heart, always; love and patience.

Hold them very tight.

They rule over life/over everything/.

Patience, You Saved Me

Patience, you saved me so many times,

But in the end, I was weak.

I even had no strength to ask.

I'm very tired from working so hard.

Please know, I will not forget your words.

I will not forget your partners.

I love them all, your family,

Wisdom, prudence, and knowledge!

No One Loves the Broken People

No one loves the broken people.

Everyone loves the successful people.

Alas, you don't know what

Your next turn may be in life!

I wish you could feel

The pain of broken people, and

Understand it is life.

Fall down, rise,

Don't depress the broken people.

They're being tested.

Don't rely on successful people.

They're being tested, too.

Different test: fall down and rise.

Life will test both.

Who deserves to fall?

Who deserves to rise?

You Were My Best Friend

You were my best friend.

You were my trust.

You told me, "You're the only one, the best!"

I was happy for your success.

I was happy for your partners.

And now, they're the best.

The success changed you,

Changed your friends.

I wish you all the best!

What I know, you never were the best.

You never were my friend.

Your partners will soon know it also.

You Wanted to Tell Me Something

You wanted to tell me something.

But I couldn't wait.

I don't know what it is.

Maybe it's not sweet news?

Maybe it's better to wait?

You want to tell me something?

Please tell me.

You're probably afraid to disappoint me,

Or maybe you want to protect me?

Please tell me.

I can't wait.

Was I right or was I wrong?

You tell me, please.

Time Is a Powerful Thing

Time is a powerful thing.

Power is time.

Never will anything happen,

Without a right time.

Negative thinking is wrong, not time.

Time has a great power.

Our impatience is a foe of time.

We must learn how

To wait, wait, and wait.

Even small foes press on..

Nothing will be late.

It seems that the time may not be so powerful.

Time is power, it's always right.

We are impatient!

The Human Beings

The human beings have emotions and feelings.

Hardest to repair is the broken heart.

It's not easy to change the mind.

But it is hard also to forgive

Arrogance and pride.

The person should try to change, not only his or her style,

The person should to change the proud heart!

You Want to See Me

You want to see me,

But you have no courage.

You want to talk to me,

But you don't know how to start.

You want to call me,

But you not sure who will answer.

You think of me,

And you're anxious too much.

Darling, don't worry about anything.

Everything will be the will of God!

Please Don't Think of Me

Please don't think of me.

Our thoughts have power.

Please don't talk of me,

Our words have power.

But, I cannot tell you,

To stop loving me.

Please don't!

The heart is not in my power!

Truth Is Pure

Truth is pure,

But, truth is, no one is pure.

Truth is courage,

And courage is true.

We should be strong

And reveal that untruth has

A dark spots on it.

With truth/ courage/,

We can wipe dark spots off.

We can return to the way

Truth wants us to be.

Truth will always fight for her crown.

Truth wants always to prevail and live.

Truth is pure, precious, and better

Than any sweet, untrue/ stories/.

— *Emotions* —

Truth will fight for her throne,

Earn her medal,

And show, *I'm Truth.*

.

Truth is courage;

We should love the truth

And keep her as a shining and

Pure diamond over our hearts!

Flowers Are a Beautiful Creation

Flowers are a beautiful creation.

The Earth will lose her beauty.

The gardens will lose their attraction.

The homes will lose their liveliness.

Life will lose its joy.

But, flowers will make us smile.

Flowers will make us happy.

This beauty, nature's creation, inspires

A powerfully lovely feeling,

To keep us emotionally happy.

My Eyes Couldn't Close for Many Hours

My eyes couldn't close for many hours.

My eyes just stared

I had deep emotions,

My heart felt special, like it did not have enough air.

Like a teenager, I didn't know what to do.

No experience, no knowledge,

I just adored him, and felt very loved to have him.

I just know that he will lift up my soul.

He will be my joy inside,

This little, sweet black boy

Whom I adore and want to adopt.

His round eyes, his curly hair, his soft skin,

His boundless energy just moves me inside.

— *Angela Herrick* —

No one can imagine how proud I am

To raise my black boy, to encourage him

To be intelligent and strong.

I will be his shoulder,

His supporter in everything,

We will always be dear to each other,

Special to each other.

We will have a sweet harmony, and

A good relationship of mother and son.

We will always have love!

Part III

Pain

The great art is to give no power to a deep pain,

And the pain will go easily away.

TEARS

Tears are caused by a sentimental emotion.

Tears are an expression of powerful feelings,

The tears could be an expression of a sweet joy,

A moving feeling, or a painful hurt.

They might also be an expression of regret, /remorse/.

Different types of tears have different expressions:

I am happy to see you,

I want to hug you,

I ask your forgiveness,

I miss you terribly.

They're all expressions of feelings, but sometimes

We can't summon the tears, they

Come without our permission.

They just come and never stop, tears of suffering and pain.

These are not welcome tears; they are the friends of wounds.

The tears do not stop the hurts; they just relieve

The pain for /some/ period of time.

The tears signify strong emotions and deep feelings,

Without emotional movement.

They will never come.

Tears can be bitter; they can be sweet.

They release the emotions we're feeling.

Without tears, you're living without emotions.

Emotional life is a universal collaboration

Of many great spirits.

If one spirit is out of harmony, emotions will hurt it.

The tears come then,

The tears of suffering an unharmonious spirit.

They show that

This spirit hurts your soul.

Without water, the flowers and trees won't grow.

Without tears, you won't have planted your soul.

When the soul has enough resources to grow, she stops the tears.

She doesn't need the moisture anymore.

Now her /soul/ needs only sun to grow and grow.

The tears of joy, they sparkle in the sun.

— Emotions —

It will be light without tears.

It will be joy sparkling in the sun.

Eyes will reflect emotions.

Better to have emotions, to have tears, and to have feelings,

Than to be cold as ice and unable to produce

/Any human emotions/ and never cry, never feel anything.

The soil needs water, the flowers need water,

The trees needs water; /all living creatures need water/.

But stones don't care; stones don't need water.

The stone cannot sense anything; it will be the same stone,

Never smaller or bigger.

The stone never changes, it doesn't feel destruction when it cracks.

The stone doesn't care about size—small or big.

It is just a stone. No emotions, no tears.

For human beings, the tears, they come for many reasons:

They come to make someone humble,

To make someone's tears pure,

To make someone warmer,

To make someone sweeter, lovelier, or more precious.

— Angela Herrick —

To some, tears bring a release of pain,

They have a purpose, as everything has purpose in life.

I wish everyone may have tears of joy. They are the sweetest tears,

And bring the joy of having a loved one in your life.

I saw two crystal sparkles in your eyes,

Tears that looked like sparkles of joy.

Having an emotion, a sweet feeling,

The sweet tears help you to see the soul of a loved one.

I have seen a lot of tears—without them, I wouldn't have seen anything!

If You Have No Pain

If you have no pain,

You have no love.

If you have love,

You know pain!

My Soul Cries

My soul cries.

Oh, physical pain never can compare

With pain inside.

Tolerate suffering and deep hurt,

When soul burns and soul cries.

Indescribable pain, when the soul burns,

And the spirit is not alive.

Life is torture, a painful fire.

You will be ready to give anything away,

To release your soul from the painful fire.

Oh, it deeply hurts when your soul burns.

Please never, never let my heart

Feel this pain again.

Oh God, release my soul, for

I have no more tears to cry!

Pain Is Not a Welcome Feeling

Pain is not a welcome feeling.

Pain does not come in easy installments.

Some feel pain too deep,

Some feel only a part of pain.

No one likes the pain, but

Believe that the deep pain is a

Lasting experience!

After Many Tears

After many tears, I grew.

My eyes became clearer

After many tears, I saw

A real personality.

Very hard to believe, after disappointment,

Very hard to believe, after betrayal,

Very hard to believe, after pain,

That it could happen to someone like you, now!

How Blind I Was

How blind I was, I didn't see your eyes.

How naive I was, I didn't see your pride.

How stupid I was, I didn't see your riches.

How crazy I was, to have feelings for you.

It was my foolishness, it was my fault,

Falling in love with you!

It was my big mistake, not to know you.

It was my illusion, to think you were sweet to me.

You gave me pain, the bitter side of sweet!

The Beautiful Picture

The beautiful picture, the beautiful story,

The glamorous dress, the gorgeous hair,

None of it has power over me.

I truly don't care who you love.

I truly don't believe you now!

I don't need anything from you.

My heart is free.

Do what you want to do!

You will never find real love and peace.

All your fake happiness will have an end.

And time will come for regrets,

But it will be very late.

I was late to understand the truth,

That no one loves you, only your wealth.

No one cares for you, only your money!

Revenge

Revenge.

I will emotionally kill you.

I want you to feel my pain.

I will stop your breathing.

I will make you stutter.

My body will blossom.

My body will be silky, but

You will never touch it.

I will make you die

I will emotionally kill you,

Never let you come to close.

I will make you feel the pain,

The pain that I felt.

I love justice; I love your dread.

I will reject you, as you once did me.

No more calls, I will take them.

No more notes, I will accept them.

I will emotionally kill you.

You must understand that it is

So cruel to play games with my feelings.

I want you to stop playing

The game of love!

I will emotionally kill you.

You will drink the bitter cocktail of pain,

The cocktail my rejected love.

You think I don't know your fear?

You think I don't know your fear?

I can see you never stop fearing.

You gave the power to your friends

To rule over your destiny.

You trust those whom I wouldn't ever trust.

You do it, because of the power of fear.

But when your friends betray you,

Your fear will double!

We Never Understand Each Other

We never understand each other.

Our planetary journey goes in different ways.

Why do you put your trust in stars

That do not shine your way?

I suffer from Pluto approaching

Jupiter only in your way.

I had seen Mars, and my anger grew.

Our planetary journey goes in different ways.

We are never close to Venus, and the

Sun does not shine. When we look at the sky

At the same time, there is always a cloud.

Oh dear, our planetary journey goes in different ways.

We should call Saturn to stop this disorder,

Don't continue the journey of two people

Who never understand each other.

If I would ask you to come?

If I would ask you to come?

I know you would.

If I would ask you to stay?

I know you would.

If I would ask you to love?

I know you would.

But the pain tells me

It will be more pain.

I wouldn't.

I Cry A Lot,

I cry a lot.

I thought the tears

Would help my pain.

I cry.

I thought the tears

Would be a relief of my pain.

I cry.

The tears never help.

They only show

My weakness.

I cry, even my days was good,

I cry, even my days was good.

I cry, even everything is smooth,

I cry, even I have more, what I need.

I cry; do you know why?

The pain inside don't care anything!

You cry, I cry

You cry, I cry.

Your tears moved down.

They moved so fast, and other tears

Came from your eyelashes.

I cry because you cry.

Your tears move my eyes.

Your eyes are wet, but you don't see it.

Darling, no more tears.

They never will

Wash our pain away!

You Know All My Pain

You know all my pain.

You know all my secrets,

It's hard for me to be with you.

You see me with eyes of pity.

I will cry more with you.

It's hard for me to be with you

Because you know all my secrets.

Darling, I don't want you to cry.

My pain will be healed.

I cannot see your tears.

Please don't see me!

I Need Your Trust

I need your trust.

It would relieve my pain.

I need you to believe me,

I don't need anything.

Never would anything be able to

Replace it, nor would it be

Equal or greater,

To your sweet self!

I Try to Forget Everything

I try to forget everything.

I try never remembering,

What my mind wishes to keep.

I never let my mind think about it,

But I cannot to make my heart

Abandon the memory of you.

The heart keeps pain longest..

I wish that something would take the place of the heart,

I wish that someone would be much sweeter.

I wish I could tell you to leave my heart.

I wish a new love will come and

Close the door to former things.

A new love can change the feeling, but

How I can do it in my own will?

I Am Not Able to Forgive

I am not able to forgive.

I will defend myself.

I gave my love

Which you refused.

I am never able to forget it!

I will defend myself from

Your rejection, that never will

Come to my heart again.

I gave you my love. You

Killed it with deep wounds,

And I never will be able to forget it!

I Saw You Cry

I saw you cry,

Your tears drop down your cheek.

I saw your wet eyes and your tears on your lips.

All I was watching and listening to

Was a moving speech,

After which no one was moved

To kiss you, to wipe your cheek,

To wipe your wet eyes,

To wipe your wet lips!

I Learn to Control My Emotions

I learn to control my emotions.

I learn to cry without tears.

I learn not to show my pain inside.

I learn not to scream.

I learn to suffer, to sacrifice.

I learn to meditate.

I learn not to trust, not to rely on anything or anyone

But me.

I learn my pain never can be healed

Without my loving God!

I Have a Talent to Heal Others

I have a talent to heal others.

I have a talent to inspire others.

I have a talent to give helpful advice

And to encourage others.

But nothing is left to me.

When I despair, no one there!

When I am disappointed, no one picks me up!

When I distress, no one soothes!

When I am angry, no one calms me!

I know this is my test,

But how long will I be under the pressure of this test?

How long will I fight my fights?

So, I dare to ask these questions

That only God may answer.

My Inside Complaint

My inside complaint—I lost everything.

My inside complaint—to be happy for nothing.

My inside complaint—to suffer and suffer.

My inside complaint—all too much pain.

You can cry, you can complain,

But maybe you don't know.

The complaints make us grow!

I Never Can Learn

I never can learn from someone else.

I have been through my own pain.

I have my spiritual journey;

I have my deep wounds.

I've learned how to have relief

And joy after tears.

I've learned how to live, despite my enemies.

I've learned how to fall and stand up.

I've learned how to be strong and never give up.

I've learned there's nothing I can do without God.

I've learned what life is about:

To be faithful to God!

The Pain Never Leaves My Heart

The pain never leaves my heart;

I'm always in pain.

If you would take my heart

From inside, you would see it

The pain is always there.

My heart is too weak to hold

The pain, always.

The pain never goes away.

I would love to ask God

To give me a new heart!

If I Could Start My Life Again

If I could start my life again,

I would nothing change.

My life is one, once given to me,

Only to me.

My life from above was created,

My journey of life, only for me.

It is my life, no one else's.

If I could change it, I would not be me.

Deep emotion, and pain, this life is mine.

I would change nothing.

Without pain, I wouldn't learn anything.

I am proud, not afraid, of all the pain

That heaven made for me!

The Pain Pierced My Heart

The pain pierced my heart.

My tears were bitter;

They accused me falsely.

Believe that I suffer not alone,

I suffer with my God.

My pain was a deep,

My tears were bitter,

My suffering was long.

Believe that the time makes

God very powerful.

The more you can suffer,

The more power

God will receive.

— *Emotions* —

My tears accused me falsely,

Without knowing,

That the pain was not only mine, but also God's.

His is the power now to cast and

/Sweep/ all accusers out.

The pain was not only mine.

Extremes

Extremes.

Those who have no extremes would never talk about it.

Those who won't have extremes, won't be able to learn.

My life is extremely everything.

My life is extreme of feeling. /emotions/

I hate extremes; they are a lot of pain to me.

The extremes, half who have them, die

The other half, surprisingly, can live.

The extreme of you were there, but it was never you.

The extreme of reality but that, in reality, it wasn't you.

The extremes of heaven and hell.

The extremes of you and not you.

The extremes of life and death.

The extremes of everything and nothing.

Life Never Comes Alone

Life never comes alone.

Life always shows two sides,

Two powers.

Life always teaches us bad and good.

You truly live when you learn two sides.

You can always compare.

You can always tell that

I already was there!

You can always tell

I know what it is to be bad;

I know what it is to be good.

You never will learn from one side.

You never will be able to compare.

Life always shows a second side.

Life has two sides—the bad and the good.

— Angela Herrick —

The important thing is to give

A chance to both sides, but

Choose the right one, the good.

We truly live when

Empowered to stand up from the knee.

When you rise from low to high,

You truly live. You learn that life

Always has two sides /good and evil/.

We Came in This World

We came in this world

To have a life.

The life, from our babyhood, will make us grow.

Life will teach us all manners and skills

That we should know.

Life will always lead us to a place

Where she has COD for us!

We will meet her, welcome guests or not.

We will meet all powers and pains.

We will meet her joy and tears.

She will turn us away from all disappointments,

From darkness to light.

Life will always lead us!

Life Is Time

Life is time.

She can change anything.

And sometimes

The good will change to bad.

It was a bad time,

And life took a different side, but

Not all good can be always good.

Not all bad can be always bad.

The precious side is when

Bad was changed to good.

It was a good time of life.

Life Is a Gift of God.

Life is a gift of God.

Life has many levels.

We may be on top; we may be too low.

We may be in the middle of it.

We may be outside all of it or

Out of this world. But still to live

Life will tell us

Where we should be.

Life will show the path

Where we should go.

Sometimes you do not appreciate the road.

Sometimes you are too tired to go,

To have a pain/.

Life has patience.

Life has time.

Life comes to be with everyone,

As long you let her live!

My soul is in trouble when I see the needy and poor.

I want to ask God one question:

Why in this world did you make rich and poor? Why?

Someone has everything and other nothing? Why?

My soul is in trouble to see all of this!

Why are some on top and others too low? Why?

Oh God, where is the answer? My soul is in tears.

My soul cries when children have no food.

My soul is in trouble when I see all of this!

Oh God, where is the answer?

You created two worlds; the top should care for the bottom?

Oh Lord, there is not always balance and care; you can see it.

The balance is not fair!

I will keep asking my question: why

Does the world have rich and poor?

The scale is not fair!

My soul is in trouble when no one cares!

— *Emotions* —

I ask the Lord of heaven to take

The scales and make justice.

The world must be a place for everyone to live!

I cannot to see the hopeless poor with low spirits,

Someone should take care of them.

Oh Lord of heaven, tell me what would be my part of it?

The answer of God:

"Not everyone likes to lift up spirits, and

I'm God—I know the poor who ignore / God/."

The rich should be a help to the poor, but many forget it.

What I understand is that there always will be rich and poor

Until God enforces justice!

CHAPTER 2

What is love?

Introduction

Love—can you compare her with anything else?

I mean a love of the heart.

Many loves of different things

Have a different feelings and statements,

But only one love is real—it's a love of the heart.

Believe it or not, not everyone finds this love.

Most human beings have a love of the mind.

They think *I love it because I should*

Or because it will improve me.

One way or another, it's a statement of the mind.

Some loves are /fake/ or just empty words

That are easy to remember.

For others, it just means nothing; what is love?

— *Angela Herrick* —

However, everyone on the planet should wish to have

This precious emotion.

It's hard to find /love/ if not everyone has it!

No one can give love without having it, but

Everyone can learn the words and manners.

Love will show if it is real or fake,

Real love will go to heaven; words

And manners will stay on Earth,

In the place where it was made.

Love is a great emotion that needs only your heart.

Real love is eternal, and other love is temporary.

Love never includes unworthy things; she is greater than those.

Love from the heart is permanent.

She always wants you to be with her.

The other love will struggle with love of the heart.

Love of the heart wants only your heart.

If I were say to come, love won't listen to me.

Love, everyone deserves you; everyone desires you,

But who can receive you?

— Emotions —

Love is a feeling; she wants to feel you.

Then you will be blessed to feel this sweet feeling

In your heart,

It will be the heaven because love will

Show her power to make a loved one happy!

Love has only a sweet feeling of joy.

Love will make you the most precious person,

For she makes all her loved ones more precious.

No other love can be compared to love of the heart.

So many different feelings inspire

Different emotions, but love only sparkles in the air.

A real love is eternal.

If someone were to ask me,

"What is the better emotion in the whole of the world?"

The answer would be very simple:

Love, love, love . . . . .

Dedicated

To my eternal love,

Vera Bergh.

You're my sweet gift,

Who remains in my heart.

My sweet love, my precious soul,

Whom I love and always want to kiss.

I lean my head on the breast of my God,

And I have ecstasy.

I am blessed for all the feelings

That comes from my loving Lord,

My precious God!

Where Lives My Love?

Where lives my love? Where can I find you?

Oh love, I've been waiting for you so long.

Where lives my love?

Oh come, oh come my bliss, my love!

Love of joy, happiness, and / felicity/.

This love, for which I waited so long,

Will find open doors.

Love, for you I will burn a candle.

I will stay and tremble;

I will feel it's time for love.

My love will be real.

But now where lives my love?

Where are you traveling?

Oh come, oh come my bliss, / my felicity/.

— Angela Herrick —

Lord, you're watching me; you know me.

My soul is well only with you.

My heavenly gift is you.

Now I want to ask you one question.

How will Earthly love fill my heart

If you, /heavenly love/, are there?

Won't it always be jealous and not fit?

Oh Lord, I need a love; I need someone to see,

To touch, and to feel for.

I need someone to love.

Oh Lord, help me to understand how my heart

Will fit two loves, earthly and heavenly?

I know there is a place only for one, but

I'm human and always need more.

I was born to have someone and to be a couple.

I want to live for someone else and feel that

Someone needs me, misses me, waits for me,

Thinks of me, dreams of me, and

Longs to see and love me.

Where Lives My Love?

Where lives my love? Where can I find you?

Oh love, I've been waiting for you so long.

Where lives my love?

Oh come, oh come my bliss, my love!

Love of joy, happiness, and / felicity/.

This love, for which I waited so long,

Will find open doors.

Love, for you I will burn a candle.

I will stay and tremble;

I will feel it's time for love.

My love will be real.

But now where lives my love?

Where are you traveling?

Oh come, oh come my bliss, / my felicity/.

— Angela Herrick —

Lord, you're watching me; you know me.

My soul is well only with you.

My heavenly gift is you.

Now I want to ask you one question.

How will Earthly love fill my heart

If you, /heavenly love/, are there?

Won't it always be jealous and not fit?

Oh Lord, I need a love; I need someone to see,

To touch, and to feel for.

I need someone to love.

Oh Lord, help me to understand how my heart

Will fit two loves, earthly and heavenly?

I know there is a place only for one, but

I'm human and always need more.

I was born to have someone and to be a couple.

I want to live for someone else and feel that

Someone needs me, misses me, waits for me,

Thinks of me, dreams of me, and

Longs to see and love me.

— Emotions —

Oh Lord, please helps me to understand how it should be?

I love my Lord so much, so dearly.

My Lord is my life, my breath, my spirit, and my health.

You are my strength, my beauty, and my feeling.

Oh Lord, how will earthly love fit in with our love?

How will our feelings live in one heart?

Lord, help me to understand it!

As I get close to God, He will send me a love,

The Love /in my heart/, where the Lord lives.

God will make happy the Lord's place.

The perfect love is a love of two in one heart.

It is the love of God's choice, comfort, and happiness.

Only God will preside over my destiny.

I came to the party, and a pair of eyes was staring at me.

He was handsome and polite.

Gentle, he kissed my hand; I felt nervous.

I was very shy, but he was a man

Who knew how to treat a woman.

— *Angela Herrick* —

It looked like he knew what he was doing.

His eyes sparkled and shined.

I was thinking, *kiss only my hands, no other parts of my body*.

His touch was so warm.

I didn't want to melt at my first party.

He invited me to the dance floor; he was great on it.

His manners were very polite.

We danced and danced—the music never stopped,

Then there was a break, and he touched my waist.

I started quivering, and I was thinking *no other parts*.

He touched, but his hands

Just made me warm.

I didn't want to melt at my first party.

Sometimes I can be lost in this kind of situation.

Sometimes I don't know what to say.

I was calm, listening to his breath.

He was warm and so pleasant.

Neither one of us wanted to interrupt the silence.

I was thrilled; I thought I had finally found my love.

I thought God had heard my prayers.

I was thrilled; I thought my dreams had come true.

I thought this is my felicity; I thought

This is a real feeling; /my body was shaken/.

Oh how sweet a dream it was,

How pleasant to have had those dreams.

It was a good moment of false illusion,

Which I never suspected.

I searched for love, listening to a feeling.

He kissed my cheek; he kissed my forehead.

His kisses were more pleasant than any others.

I was just trembling; maybe he is the prince for whom

I have been waiting so long?

He took my hand and led me outside.

We went on a walk, and we stopped on the beach.

It was a beautiful evening, very romantic!

— Angela Herrick —

He held my two hands and approached to kiss me.

He tried to kiss my lips.

It was a gentle, sweet kiss.

Our bodies' shadows were on the sand beach.

And we held each other;

Two hands now were one.

An ocean was made of sounds and tides.

We were, at first sight, very romantic.

My life started in an emotional way.

I was afraid to raise my feelings.

I never thought about tomorrow; I was always happy today.

One day, he brought a beautiful flower,

And here he was of good taste.

His flowers were the most beautiful I had ever seen.

Always he found a great pick of anything,

I felt this is felicity

To have a such beautiful treatment,

To have a such beautiful things,

From a handsome, gentle man.

— Emotions —

I thought no one can be so lovely as he.

He always knew a good place to go eat,

And good things to possess and to buy.

He knew the value of the things he owned, and the quality.

But the most priceless thing of all was his kiss.

He always was so slow and gentle to

Reveal these sweet moments.

He knew all of the joys in life.

In my dreams, I was with him,

Never was thinking of anyone but him,

He needed to fill all the space of my heart and mind.

I had waited so long for felicity.

Our days seemed too short, the time flew.

We were in a different place with a beautiful environment.

Sometimes I couldn't wait for another day to see him,

To see his smile and his beauty.

I couldn't sleep, and always my thoughts were about him.

I wondered if he was not asleep at this time and if he was

Thinking or dreaming about me.

Our days, pardon, now weeks

Had been a wonderful time.

— Angela Herrick —

He invited me everyday to dinner; he was everyday

The same polite, gentle, warm man and he

Wanted always to stay a little longer before I went home.

Our evenings always were beautiful and great.

I thought I had found a long awaited answer to my feelings and felicity.

Then, after nine weeks, I was afraid to voice my feelings.

I was afraid the power of love was /what I needed,

But only with the right person/.

I was afraid to fall in love, but I couldn't control my feelings.

Now our mouths seems so short, and everything that he ordered

Was so amazingly lovely.

We had a great time. It seemed he enjoyed my company,

And always gently he kissed my hand when it was time to leave.

He kissed my cheek so warmly,

I thought this was the felicity for which I had waited so long.

Now eight months later, he was the same as always,

Inviting me to dinner and to other places.

I had grown emotionally in our romance—

— Emotions —

It had been over eight months now—
A wonderful time it was!

One night I was asking myself, *What is this relationship about?*
He had never told me the words, "I love you!"
He never proposed to marry me.
What is this relationship about?
I was thinking deeply, despite my risen emotions,
That this must be our goal, we cannot forever
Only share the table for dinner.

I don't know what this relationship is about?
I don't know how to ask?
Whenever I was in a difficult/stupid situation, my wisdom led me
To the spiritual power, to my greatest Lord, my mighty God.

Oh Lord, no one knows better than you, everything and anything,
No one has power and dominion over human beings like you do.
No one can be my advisor, my counsel, and my comfort like you.

Oh Lord, did I almost fall in love with a handsome,
Gentle, polite, and rich man,
Who treats me very well, who comes to me in my dreams?

Oh Lord, sometimes I melt from his kisses,

From his lovely touches.

He is the one for whom I was waiting so long.

/My felicity/, maybe he is my prince?

Oh Lord, help me to find the answer, help me!

Lord, You know all hearts; You know all thoughts.

Please help me, dearest God, whom I love more

Than earthly attachments.

Oh God, please control my human nature, my human emotions

Control my mind, my deeds, and my life.

Oh God, I trust You! Give me the answers please?

God's answer, "My child, I heard your prayers,

And your concern,

I heard your questions, my child—be strong!

This is not an equally financial relationship;

His family devotes the money."

Thank you, my Lord, /for this answer/.

I understand that we have different values of life.

We're even looking

Differently in an emotional way.

My night was so long, longer than you can imagine.

I thank God for being my counsel.

However, I haven't yet had an answer to my other questions.

Why does God make my heart,

So warm?

One night cannot give you all the answers

Or change your heart.

The next day, he invites me to the beautiful park.

I was so glad to be in such a beautiful place.

He always looked the same, his emotions

Invisible, covered in thick ice.

But he is so gentle, educated, well-mannered, and

He knows /how to treat a woman/.

He knows how to control his cold, trained mind.

He knows what he wants, he doesn't let

His feelings rise up, out of control.

He never gives power to love

It will destroy his money, his empire.

It will destroy his financial statements, his mind as bank!

Thanks to God, I see his entire fake cover complex.

He does what he wants to have a great time

With a woman, who nothing claims!

Except he doesn't know that she can fall in love.

He never talks about it.

He doesn't know that the woman who walks with him

Is waiting for love so long in her life…

I understand we need to talk; I cannot walk with a man

Who keeps me as a pet dog, who he

Very beautifully treats, walks, and feeds.

I need more than that; I need a priceless thing,

I need love!

How do I start to talk, to ask him this important question?

Oh Lord, help me!

I suggested sit on a bench, and when I took more air, more oxygen,

I started to talk.

I have to question you; please answer me.

"What is your question?"

What is love?

— *Emotions* —

He was calm, and then he looked at me like I was from another planet.

I was waiting for his answer; he didn't know what to say.

This is the answer: he doesn't know anything about love.

I ask again, "What do you know about love?"

He said, "What love? What do you mean, 'what is love?'"

I answered, "I know about love, about the feeling at heart.

I always dreamed about love; my heart is formed for love."

I answered, "Love is a feeling of the heart, when someone

Cannot live without you,

When someone wants you for the rest of life,

When someone would even be ready to die for you,

When someone will miss you and always love you!

Love is a sweet spirit from above/ that lives at heart/."

He was listening and tried to learn new skills,

A new education.

But love is naturally comes from above.

"Sorry!"—he said, "I truly don't know anything about feelings,

Financial freedom drives me.

Should I die?—Now?"

No honey, you can live as long as you wish /or want/.

You can be free, but you will never find the gift of love,

And love will never find you!

The most grievous deal in the world is

To have money and no love!

You gain money, but without love, you gain nothing!

Please think for one moment,

You have wealth and no Love!

What is better?

Two Stars

Heaven is a blue universe that has
A many different heavenly bodies:
Stars, comets, meteors, messier and constellations..
The luminous light turns the heavens
Into an incredible universal beauty. When stars are exposed
To light, it makes for magical nights.
We can see numerous stars, but we're never able to count
Or know which stars will shine in heaven forever.
All stars have names, nicknames, all stars in heaven have
Different lights, as a human bodies have emotions.

The stars in heaven look for harmony,
The universal harmony of light,
As human beings look for harmony of the soul, too.
The stars have a dozen choices in heaven,
But from billions of choices, the one star wants to have
The same harmony as the heavenly bodies.
They want the star who will be the one.

The star is a heavenly body, as all living bodies are.

They're breathing, they're having movements.

All heavenly bodies were created in a mysterious way,

The way of lights, the way of miracles, fires, storms, or

Seasons of change.

So many different ways comes from nature/creation/.

All heavenly creatures have specific bodies, never would two be the same.

Everything in the world is a different creation.

One emotion has power over everything—

It is a precious emotion, love!

One Star watches another with a

Bright smile, the light cast sparkles on her face.

The star looks so beautiful in her blue sparkles

With a silver shade. The star is very social; her name is Acomodia.

Acomodia starts to blink her light on one sweet star whose name is Vestoria.

They find a common light

That attracts and makes them brighter and brighter.

The two stars can see each other very often now,

They cast light on each other.

— *Emotions* —

Acomodia spins around to see Vestoria.

They now never pay any attention to passing comets or meteors.

,Only when a space is open do the two stars

Feel a warm connection.

Out of the billions of other stars, they want to see only each other.

Sometimes a luminous light blocks the view,

Sometimes Vestoria must turn her face away from the light,

Around her, away from other heavenly bodies.

When the view is open; Vestoria can see to Acomodia,

In her open space of heaven now.

Two stars in space look for each other.

Two stars among a billon heavenly bodies

Found an electrical, warm connection in heaven now.

Vestoria and Acomodia are luminous

When they smile to each other.

They know the change of days to nights,

They have their own radial position.

They can see each other.

Vestoria disappeared when lightning bolt came.

She was under the smoke of lighting bolt and

The deep sound of the thunderstorm's power.

Acomodia patiently waited for

Lighting bolt's action to be done.

Two stars, out of billons of others,

Who at first smiled to each other,

Were waiting to see each other

In open space. Now, they want more.

Two stars now start to care for each other in this cosmic space.

When lighting bolt is close, or wind or thunder

Storm comes with strong clouds, the two stars worry for each other.

How did they find each other?

What have they found they have in common?

Vestoria was close with many attractive stars,

But she didn't even see them.

Vestoria desired to see only Acomodia,

Who was two miles away!

That distance was full of different stars,

But she desired to see only the one, her Acomodia.

Heavenly love is higher, and the distance

Of connection immeasurable.

Love has no measure, no limit, and no prediction—anywhere!

Two stars were happy to see each other from a long distance.

Two stars among billons were able to see

Each other with a special light that was unlike

Any other light in heaven.

The light was composed of special beams,

Unrecognizable to all the other billons of stars.

The light was special—it was a light of love,

That never reveals its secret..

The key of love—to ignite light and love of heaven—

Has a color, a special shine, for only two stars.

Now we know how two stars can be recognizable to each other,

It is a special light, Vestoria shines on Acomodia and

Acomodia shines on Vestoria with

A light that no other stars have.

Yes-every heavenly body has individual sparkles,

Individual lights.

Out of billons stars, only the stars meant for each other

Can see the same light .

Acomodia and Vestoria share the same energetic

Nature, and they have a same power of light.

The other neighbors have lower powers or higher,

But never the same.

From the beautiful light that Acomodia

Shone on her, Vestoria became brighter and more beautiful.

The same happened to Acomodia,

Who loves that luminous game.

She loves her luminous dance, which made her more attractive and lovely.

The two stars were happy and they

Brightened heaven with their light..

The two stars had fallen in love.

Love in heaven—it is a wonderful happiness.

Love is a happiness everywhere!

Acomodia, in love, made her brightness so great

That many other stars around here could feel this brightness

And see her light.

Many stars around Acomodia were much shinier now

Because her light of love made other stars shine, too.

— *Emotions* —

From one happy star, the happiness spread to many other stars.

From one love, the love was extended to others everywhere.

Love has magical key—to make everyone happy all around, without limit,

/On earth or in heaven/.

Vestoria saw that Acomodia was making

Her neighbors' stars smile brighter.

Vestoria saw that light

Shine on the faces of her neighbors.

It was parade of light.

Love from one can make a dozen happy, and

Light of love can give the light to millions of other stars.

This is really heaven!

But, too many stars were shining bright from

Acomodia's light of love, and Vestoria had to consider

If these would be a problem for her.

You see, Vestoria wants to be the only light of joy for her Acomodia.

She wants to share the magical light of electricity with her partner.

Vestoria was feeling jealous.

Vestoria likes to see her Acomodia with a special light.

But, from two miles away, she wants no one else to have it.

Vestoria is afraid that the luminous feast of bright stars will swallow Acomodia.

Vestoria is also feeling scared that she might lose her love one, Acomodia.

Vestoria is worried that someone may steal or destroy their relationship.

Acomodia took Vestoria to the luminous light to dance.

They feel happiness and joy together.

Nothing can be greater than finding your mate, your dance partner.

Dance has a power of joy, when you dance with

A loved one you can forget all your worries.

Acomodia loves to dance with her Vestoria

All night, and never see the changes in heaven.

Vestoria is deeply in love with her Acomodia;

She has a feeling now that her light is stronger than any other light in heaven.

— *Emotions* —

She feels her light is so strong; it is like having fire inside.

Vestoria is an educated star, but wanting to control her light,

She starts to study again.

Poetically, she thinks, two stars, two loves, two lights;

It would be nice to unite two loves into one!

Two stars find a love.

Acomodia, from her luminous light, looks like pure crystal.

Vestoria, from her luminous light, looks like a

Bohemian crystal, with blue and silver sparkles.

Vestoria feels her light so bright that she feels a strong pressure of gas.

Soon she will not be able to control the fire inside her.

Vestoria gives power over to love; her body starts to burn from

The light of love; inside she feels fire.

Vestoria knows that she loves Acomodia with all her power now.

Vestoria thinks that it is her destiny,

To marry Acomodia.

Vestoria wants Acomodia forever.

And soon she plans a proposal to Acomodia.

Acomodia is happy with a bright light that surrounds her every night.

She loves luminous dance and happy time.

Acomodia is the star of the party; she likes to see many smiles.

She is a social star.

In happy moments, the happy hours occupy Acomodia's happy life.

Acomodia is in love with Vestoria; she feels the special light.

Heaven has no time, no age, no years;

And the key of eternity, the key of life is love.

Without love, heaven won't be a live space.

Without love never will anyone be born a new life.

Vestoria, deeply in love with Acomodia,

Never imagines any better choice,

Of all the billons of stars,

Than to be with her Acomodia only.

Vestoria has a picture and a dream of their wedding.

She will invite many other stars.

She will invite meteors and comets also.

She will invite the crescent moon, who will bring a wreath of her blessing.

— *Emotions* —

Vestoria is excited to think about the entire guest list.

Vestoria thinks that her wedding will be brighter and happier

Than any other wedding in heaven.

Vestoria dreams of her wedding and her Acomodia forever.

They will be partners forever, and she will have Acomodia in her radius,

Not two miles away.

Vestoria thinks that what's best is to have

A loved one close and forever.

Acomodia is enjoying her emotional happiness.

That Vestoria loves and cares for her so much,

Makes Acomodia's light beam.

She never feels far from her loved one.

When two stars have sparkles, happiness, closeness,

They are in love in heaven, making all of heaven

Bright and happy now.

Then heaven starts a rumor that Vestoria wants to be

Closer to Acomodia, that she loves her and wants to

Marry to her loved one.

Heaven knows in advance that Vestoria will

Choose the bright night for their wedding time.

Vestoria writes the proposal note to Acomodia to marry her.

Her note reads, *My light belongs to you now.*

My life is you, in all heaven I love only you.

Acomodia, will you marry me?

After Vestoria writes her proposal, she

Calls her good friend, Meteor!

Meteor is very glad to help his friend Vestoria

Deliver her note to Acomodia.

Meteor goes with a cosmic speed,

Flying like a rocky missile,

To see Acomodia and give her a note from Vestoria .

Meteor knows it is a special note, that it has a red and

Pink ribbons and sparkles around it.

While Meteor delivers

Vestoria's proposal,

Vestoria awaits the answer.

If this time were measured on Earth,

It would be two seconds.

— Emotions —

But Vestoria is very nervous and spins around
Her orbit ninety-nine times in two seconds.
For Vestoria, the two seconds are an eternity.

Love created deep pressure sometimes.
The emotions drive everything in unpredictable ways.
Love is a most powerful emotion!
Love moves the universe.

Acomodia sees that Meteor is approaching her
With something in his hands that
Looks so beautiful.
Meteor gives the note to Acomodia, saying,
"This is made for you by Vestoria."

Acomodia smiles and replies, "Thank you!"
She pulls out two beautiful ribbons, red and pink,
And start to read the note from her Vestoria.
Acomodia reads and is happy, to hear that she is the light of Vestoria's life.
But when she reads the end of the note about marriage,
There is a big change in her brightness.

Acomodia isn't prepared; she isn't ready for those last words.
She did not expect any changes in her life, but this

Note from Vestoria asking her to marry causes

Acomodia to lose her shine; she rapidly changes her light.

The words "to marry" scare her

And push her back.

She does not want to lose her space where she is happy,

Where she has a luminous dance every night in her orbit.

Acomodia does not want to lose her independence;

She is happy with what she has; she is not ready to change anything.

To marry means to lose my freedom, to lose my social life,

To lose the heavenly parties, Acomodia thinks.

She wants to keep Meteor a little longer and longer,

Then she just gives him Vestoria's proposal note.

Vestoria has a sweet intention to give Acomodia all her light,

All her brightness, all her fire, everything that she has to give,

And make one star in the universe.

She loves her with all her power and light.

Vestoria made her proposal note not in one day or one night.

She feels fire inside; she cannot hold out so long and suffer.

Vestoria thinks it is the right time to have her partner for all her life.

Vestoria has a pure intention of eternity and the feeling of love.

It is Vestoria's dream to unite the lights of love in marriage.

She dreams to be near her loved one every night,

To have her close and forever.

Of all the billons of stars in the universe

Only Acomodia was able to ignite her light,

Her fire.

When Meteor brings back

The proposal note to Vestoria

Vestoria feels her fire go out;

Acomodia does not wish to marry her.

Vestoria holds her note, trying to control her emotions.

She takes time to understand that the

Deep emotion of love is now turning to pain.

Love is a great light that makes all stars much brighter.

Love moves the universe, but when light has no power,

The heaven feels pain.

Love desires eternity, eternity of light, eternity of heaven.

Love desires joy and happiness, not pain.

But when your partner has an opposite vision,

The pain of it may destroy the light.

It sees no future in heaven.

Vestoria is deeply depressed now.

She has lost her gleam of light, her bohemian, crystal face,

Is awash in gray clouds of pain.

Vestoria is no longer able to see sparkles of universe.

It is an entire space of clouds now.

Her shining glow slowly, slowly starts to vanish.

Like an aging crystal, she begins to crumble.

The fire she once felt inside, takes a turn in the opposite direction,

That no one ever wishes for, because it begins to burn her.

The fire that was once of love, is now a fire of pain.

Vestoria lets her fire burn her.

Without Acomodia she lets herself die.

Vestoria without Acomodia doesn't wish to live,

— Emotions —

She wants her fire to turn into a blaze,

Leading to entire darkness, no power of joy or happiness.

Vestoria would never be able to fall in love after her experience of pain.

Without love, she sees no sense in living.

Vestoria lets her fire burn, and she vanishes from heaven.

Without the power of light, heaven has no power of the life.

Just before Vestoria vanishes, before her death brings her to the edge,

Vestoria seeks a final wish, an answer to a question.

She will give half of the universe to the one who can answer this question:

/What is eternal love?

Among the billons of stars, I believe that a million vanish quickly,

But the rest vanish slowly.

Some stars never find love in heaven and

They disappear. Others find love, but they will die from it.

I will give half of the universe to the person who can answer this question,

Which love will stay in heaven forever?

Every day and night, some stars are born while some die.

Love has extremes: happiness or sadness,

Joy or pain, Light or dark, Life or death.

Love is fire. The varying power of each fire,

/That has an appoint future/.

Vestoria, now very weak,

Tries to find an answer, even though she has chosen

To die for her loved one.

But now, she complains, asking

Where is path for the light? Where does Love desire to be in the universe?

Where is the key to finding a loved one forever?

How can you be with your loved one forever?

Vestoria, now screaming loudly with her last power.

Who can have eternal, desirable love and forever?

As the light of her life turns more and more to darkness,

She has dark color now.

The last word she pronounces, barely audible now, is "love."

— *Emotions* —

Her light disappears and the star vanishes forever.

No one in heaven ever was able to answer her questions.

All the billons of stars of the universe, but none were able to provide an answer to

"What is eternal love?"

A MIRACLE CAN HAPPEN

Two precious women met each other.

Before that, for a very long time, they needed each other.

For a very long time, they desperately sought each other.

This took them not one day or a few nights,

I would say it took them a half their lives.

However, as it happens now, after a long time of searching,

They met each other after many strides,

After many obstacles.

They were confident and sure,

"If this is meant to be, it will happen."

They found each other, they did it.

But they never escaped the other questions.

Is this the right time?

How would we fit in?

— *Emotions* —

One of these precious ladies, we'll call Wealth,

The other precious Lady, we'll call Love.

They desired each other, but two powers have different impulses.

Two powers have a completely different sense of life.

One power, wealth, has many possessions.

The other power, love, is characterized by enormously deep emotions.

The two ladies are very beautiful in appearance and attitude!

From a distance, you might say that they would never be independently happy.

From up close, you might wonder if they'd be happier alone.

All life with love becomes very sweet on Earth,

And Earth becomes a happy place to live.

Love has the power to fill all bodies with sweet air

And all eyes with many sparkles.

Love fills the heart with joy and comfort.

Love keeps the body in bloom and the face smiling.

Love will never let heavy or sad energy to come in your mind.

Love is a great healer..

Love wants joy in all hearts, wherever life accepts it..

Love protects loved ones from danger and protects against all enemies.

Love adores all fine things and gives good gifts to loved ones.

Love is a gifted that can be given and received.

Love has the power to never leave a loved one under any circumstances.

Love wishes to be eternal.

The precious Lady Joy, who comes only

To chosen and desirable people,

Never, ever disappoints anyone.

Everyone who keeps company with Lady Love will always be blessed.

By Lady Joy's presence as well.

Joy and Love make their chosen ones very lucky.

Love is everything, beauty, happiness, joy, inner comfort,

Sweetness, and desire to live.

Love moves all emotions.

Love lives in everything and everyone.

― Emotions ―

Love, with her power, can put the broken back together.

Love's power will restore all.

Love's power will heal all.

Love's power will keep you living longer and feeling younger.

Love is inner peace and happiness in solitude.

Love is the most precious in the whole universe, all who

Search for her find her someday.

Love extends her beauty over nature; she covers the ground

With beautiful flowers.

Love has compassion and kindness.

This precious Lady Love has only one rule;

She comes only to those who desire and like her.

Love doesn't keep company in unpleasant

Environments or waist time with discomfort.

If Love comes, she makes only harmony

If she loves, she makes only happiness.

Without love—no one, ever, would be happy,

No one would know joy or paradise.

The universe is a great collaboration of numerous things.

The universe has many powers over many objects.

You can easily see beauty in the work of precious Lady Love.

Before Lady Love exposes her power, she

Carefully searches for the right place.

Love exposes her power when she has confidence.

The power of love is the power of happiness.

The universe hides Lady Love.

I would say she is not in a visible place; it is not easy to find her.

Love travels so many routes that when someone searches

For her in some / specific/ place, she may be not there.

Love can be close to you, and then, just to change

The way, she distances herself.

Do you really need Lady Love and want her?

Or do you need more time?

Or do you wish you had a little bit more time to wait?

Love must be assured that you love,

Desire, and want her forever.

In search of universal love, you might travel a long time

And the path may never be made right.

— Emotions —

Love may have missed you when you were there.

Do you know why?

Love has a strong feeling about whom to approach.

Only the right one with her good power and good energy,

For she wouldn't give anything to anyone who wasn't ready or who didn't deserve it.

Lady Love looks for all the answers and makes the right decisions.

Lady Love wants to make her loved ones happy.

Her choices must be careful and right.

Many years with Lady Love will be like

One special year, combining all the sweet joy and true happiness of life.

When the two ladies met each other, they were astonished.

They thought they had found paradise on Earth.

But one question kept coming to mind—was this the right time?

The two ladies were on one route, which is very unusual.

Not often can you see this path—it happens once per century.

Lady Love and Lady Wealth in one path—one harmony.

The two ladies were the exception and the sensation of this universal journey.

But it happens—this very unusual conjunction.

They've met each other, and I would say they're

Both wishing and /desiring/ it.

Lady Wealth spent twenty years of her fanatical work—

Everyday, seventeen hours per day, nonstop—

Without resting or relaxing.

With no peace of mind, ever.

Lady Wealth has the power to possess everything,

The finest things, but she always wants better and more.

Always wants to be greater and greatest, always desires more chances,

More opportunities, and more of everything.

Lady Wealth flaunts her power with her great possessions.

Wealth has luxury and servants.

Wealth loves when you serve her; she rewards it.

Wealth has everything except time. /She hasn't / enough.

It is grievous when wealth has no time to enjoy..

Wealth has power to buy anything, to enslave anyone.

Wealth likes to rule as queen.

Wealth likes to show off, "I can have everything."

Emotions

But Wealth looks so sad when her heart is empty.

She has everything,

But she can't put any of it in her heart.

She feels alone; she suffers.

The powerful Lady Wealth often has to cover up her emptiness.

Her heart—she pull strings to feel anything,

But she feels nothing, just empty and hurt.

Her heart feels a lack of joy, but her eyes

Can see all beautiful things and

Her eyes are always happy.

Lady Wealth is afraid to confess,

"I have everything, but always I feel it is not enough for me!"

Lady Wealth, she doesn't need good treatment—she has it.

Lady Wealth doesn't need good gifts—she has them.

Lady Wealth doesn't need a good time—she has it.

Lady Wealth doesn't need more friends—she has them.

Lady Wealth, alone, never would be a happy person.

She is searching for love.

Love alone has a chance to be happy,

But not Wealth, alone.

Love is joy and happiness at heart, but Wealth

Feels emptiness and loneliness at heart.

Love has better chance to be happy without all that luxury.

Lady Wealth doesn't know any other power; she just works all these twenty years,

And has not realized the true happiness of life.

Wealth keeps working always; she has no time to consider it.

She keeps going with her casual friends who like to keep her company, always.

When Lady Wealth is generous, she throws a great party.

Everyone has a good time with her.

Wealth shows her power and throws a good party, but after,

When her friends go home to a loved one,

Wealth feels an emotional gap—

On the exterior she feels happiness, but she never feels it inside.

Lady Wealth never talks about her feelings to anyone.

She never opens this

Deep, inside secret to anyone.

You just think that she is happy, that publicly she wishes it.

Wealth never opens her heart; she keeps it closed with a large padlock.

Wealth never allows to anyone to open her padlock,

Nor does she like to talk about it.

Emotions

It is her deep secret, but she likes to think that she is happy always.

Only, Wealth forgot, or doesn't know, what Love

Knows better than anyone.

Love knows the pure truth.

Without Love, Wealth is miserable and unhappy.

But Wealth is strong; she waits for her opportunity; she always has hope for it.

Wealth has pride; she never talks about miserable things, about feelings.

She doesn't like to disappoint anyone, and what she most fears

Is that she will destroy herself emotionally.

The Lady Wealth is great, powerful lady,

Who presides over many things

On Earth But without love,

She must pretend to blossom every year, every season.

Wealth tries never to talk about emotions; they may cost her high price.

She is careful to keep it all inside.

Lady Wealth, who is so precious inside, is very beautiful outside.

She is very pretty; she knows how to properly treat her body,

But without love, she is an existence of expensive things.

The universe has compassion, and tolerates this crime of

Wealth without Love.

The universe gives a chance, just once, so that Wealth and Love

May meet.

Two ladies meet each other, two powers you can see and feel.

Nothing in the whole universe would be so precious as to have this perfect match.

Never has any harmony of any jewels in the universe ever been greater

Than the harmony of Wealth and Love.

Can you imagine the thrill of the universe?

Can you imagine the miracle that is about to happen?

The universe waited so long for this harmony!

An impossible thing happening in the universe proves that

Nothing is impossible.

Miracles are always possible.

Maybe only once in century, but Wealth did meet Love.

The Wealth understands that the time is right,

She cannot wait any longer; she spent twenty years

Searching for love, hoping it would come one day.

— *Emotions* —

The Wealth felt it was the right time. She needed love.

So she wishes to spend every night to be with her Lady Love.

Wealth knows, now her nights won't

Be loneliness and emptiness at heart.

Wealth is the lady of wisdom; she only wished a real love.

Here is the test she used to prove it:

Lady Wealth would not believe sweet words only.

She would not believe smiles only.

She would not believe one opinion—she needed two or three.

She needed proof of everything and time to consider everything.

Wealth never came easily enough to believe anything.

Sometimes her behavior was stubborn; she has always her way.

Sometimes she refused to open her eyes to see the truth.

Sometimes she was tired and could not make right decision.

Sometimes she wanted to take more time.

Wealth needs more time than anyone in universe

To make her choices.

No one likes to be ridiculed.

No one, in all the universe, needs a longer time

To make a decision than Wealth.

It not easy for Wealth to decide

And to be sure if it's really love.

Wealth will, many times, pull on Love,

And then she will regret it, but it will be too late.

Or she might forget about Love,

And she would struggle emotionally.

Doubt is the same as no choice.

Doubts make Wealth alone again.

Struggling with doubts

Always causes her another problem: fear.

Fear makes Wealth feel more alone than anyone.

Fear makes her unhappy.

Lady Wealth, terrified at the risk of losing

What she has in /her possession/,

Lives with a double-edged sword;

One side of her power is in very strong possession of everything.

The other side lives in fear of losing it all.

Fearful Lady Wealth cannot have joy or peace in her heart—

Nor can she have serenity of the mind.

She is always under pressure, never free.

— *Emotions* —

Only Lady Love knows the key to happiness and peace.

Two precious ladies, both can hold each other up.

Love will show her power—will cast all fear out!

Love is stronger than any destruction.

Love always shoulders and supports her love one.

Love will bring peace and comfort to her love one.

Love will keep the mind free from anxiety.

Wealth needs stimulus; Love needs feeling.

Many times, Wealth makes wrong choice because

The tension and fear were very deep and strong.

Sometimes Wealth has confidence in things

That do not deserve her attention at all.

Wealth hates losses.

Wealth always counts everything.

The Wealth loves to buy everything, except

She forgets, or she doesn't know, that

The priceless thing cannot be possessed.

Wealth will mock up if she tries to buy Love.

She thinks she can buy everything on Earth, but

Real Love cannot be bought!

Love is a priceless thing. Money cannot to do it!

Money is no security for hearts.

Wealth wishes to have joy; she wishes to take it easy in life,

But great possessions keep her power.

The scariest thing for Wealth, if she picks Love, is

To have a trusting partner.

Wealth understands that business always needs

Partners, but you can't always trust—there is always risk.

Sometimes Wealth may meet with pain; the partner can betray her,

Use others just for her own purpose.

The Lady Wealth tearfully questions, *Why me?*

This deceitful world cannot really make Lady Wealth happy.

No one, most of time, cares about her feelings.

The partners care about her checks and money.

Wealth has a bitter experience of disappointments, betrayals, and losses.

The Wealth has pain with no appreciation.

She may turn to the bitter side of life;

She will try to escape all inner discomfort, all pressure,

All disappointment.

Emotions

Lady Wealth may try to change partners, but it would only cause more pain.

Lady Wealth is very pretty, on the outside, but always has inner pain and discomfort.

Pain makes the pretty Lady of Wealth late, makes her look different,

And causes her beautiful face to show many nervous lines and wrinkles.

Lady Wealth, as all ladies of the universe, wishes to be happy,

To have joy, but Wealth will never be able to do it, alone. It /would be emptiness/.

Once in a hundred years, the universe can show that nothing is better for

Wealth than to meet her love.

The miracle happens once, even after twenty years, or later in life.

But it does happen.

Meeting Lady Love is never too late—better late, than never!

Lady Love doesn't care about age.

Lady Love doesn't care about previous pains; she knows she can heal.

Love can wipe off tears.

Love can lift the wounded soul.

Love can bind broken hearts.

Love knows disappointment is not forever.

These two precious ladies need each other in life.

Wealth may have a sad life without ever meeting her love.

Wealth may have a fatal end, after betrayals or great loses.

Her protective power would be her love.

Wealth alone would look very miserable after getting everything out.

It would be very sad for Wealth to think about it—

Better never to think or talk about

Bankruptcy or sudden losses.

The mind will feel hard pressure,

Wealth might, after her losses, lose her mind.

The universe has deep compassion and will open the door,

Sending Wealth to redemption.

It is only one way to send love!

Nothing will come by itself, should Wealth wish it.

Wealth should wish for security of the mind and heart,

And always, she should ask heaven for a real love.

— *Emotions* —

Then the universe would make the impossible possible, opening the path

For Wealth to meet Love!

Everything in life, unfortunately, takes time.

Everything needs patience and zeal to achieve; but never

Lose hope that the miracles can happen—sooner or later.

In life, two powers will meet each other.

Believe it or not,

Wealth always has time to meet her love.

Love is compassion.

Love heals all wounds.

Wealth can only be happy with Lady Love—there she

Finds an inner comfort and a peaceful mind.

Those who never give the universe a chance,

Or who were headed in wrong direction,

Will not be happy without love.

Wealth needs Love more than anyone in universe.

The universe likes surprises, so let the miracle happen,

And let improbable powers perform it.

Everything has power; the sweetest is love.

Love's power will show her truth.

Love has a very deep emotional value.

Love cares for hearts and minds, and for the health of all the body.

Love has joy that will show on the outside, and

She rewards loved ones with happiness.

These two precious ladies—they're both powerful and beautiful.

They both should be happiest.

Wealth without love would never be happy,

Wealth with Love only

Would be emotionally safe and mentally secure.

Their beauty will never disappear; it will only grow and grow.

Love is nature; like flowers, she will flourish

With her loved one, each season of each year.

These two precious ladies meet each other once every

Hundred years.

I wish many, many times

That Wealth could meet her love sooner.

Emotions

The universe has a path for everyone,

But happiest is Wealth when she meets Love.

Everyone wishes to have a happy life.

The miracle can happen.

Nothing is better than when Wealth and Love harmonize.

The universe would thrill forever!

Joy of Love

Real love is a precious emotion.

Love's power is a force to be reckoned with.

Love won't listen to any advice.

Love waits for her action, her impulse, to have what she desires.

Everything in the world has two sides /positive and negative.

Love is no exception/.

Deceitful love is blind—with a seductive air, she attracts the wrong partner.

After a time, this soft, deceitful air would finally disappear.

Love has her weak moments.

Love would be weakest with a wrong choice; she would be blind, and

She would not see reality for a while.

The reality is that the sparkles on air

May have seduced love for a while.

The real test of love of is suffering.

Emotions

Love tests her pain, for those who survive

Will receive her rewards.

Love without test may meet only pain.

How did I learn love was approaching me?

It happened twice in different ways.

One began in sparkles—it was a blaze that left only ashes. And in the end

There was pain.

The second time, it started from pain,

An emotional war.

I wasn't expecting anything; I didn't know what would happen in the end.

I never expected the sweet end!

How, from a deep, emotional suffering,

How, from deep wounds, refusals, and misunderstandings,

How, impatience and distress,

How, from soul's tears,

How, from disappointments,

How, from a deep and tolerant pain at heart,

Love can survive and hang on until the sweet end?

— Angela Herrick —

I never did understand that real love is never able to

Disappoint anyone, after all of it.

Love likes the test.

Not ready to meet the pain, who can prepare

For it and just walk away?

No one likes to suffer or know the sense of it.

Real love has a real path to see joy.

The reality of real love would last forever.

Whoever cannot prepare for pain

Would just leave or walk away and never be able to see

And understand real love.

No one loves to suffer, but you should know

The suffering will make your love eternal.

Love always has a test, you should listen to

Your heart, where love likes to dwell.

Never fail at heart; if there is pain, love will do her work.

No one can take your heart and leave you with an empty space.

Time will heal pain and you will

Experience love, you will grow after suffering.

— *Emotions* —

Believe that love must to have roots at heart; if there were only air it

Would be not enough; suffering plants roots.

Deep suffering plants even deeper roots.

Do you need to sacrifice and suffer for love's eternal roots?

No, the tears will produce roots.

No one was born with roots of love.

The time and suffering will have planted this root, making love eternal.

Believe that eternal love is not for everyone.

All suffering has difficult tests and needs a great knowledge.

Suffering without forgiveness would never be

Without compassion, kindness, patience, and humility.

Never would harmony bring us to that last level.

Harmony of love is eternity of universe.

The suffering should prevail over all painful pressures,

Over all wounds that you never would expect to surface.

Don't let impatience take power

To say, "I cannot take it anymore," or "I cannot—

I leave right now!"

This suffering may bring pain with much hurt.

You should know it's a test of love, and we need to be humble about it.

All pain can be healed, just use the weapons of forgiveness and kindness.

Love comes with suffering for one purpose: she wants to be eternal.

Not everyone can endure the test of love—only the chosen one might manage it.

Love knows everyone hearts; she will choose, for her

Eternity, her chosen one.

Love has the most tolerated pain in the universe.

How deep the pain of love can be, how sweet her joy.

Love tests many times the feeling of the hearts.

The longer the suffering, the more chance to eternity.

Love without tears withers the flowers.

Flowers always need water to grow.

The more tears, the more the flowers of love will grow.

Love is suffering and pain.

Love is tears, hurts, and painful feelings. But

After pain comes a sweet joy.

Love is the most precious emotion, the most precious thing; it is priceless.

— *Emotions* —

Love wants to be eternal.

Sometimes you're exhausted and don't believe

It will come, ever.

The pain makes you weak, you lose faith or

Hope. You have no strength,

Nothing left. The suffering took everything out of you.

The tears will take away all pressure, like

A grape pressed hard, there will one day be wine. /Juice of joy/.

After pain, the law of heaven was made into joy.

Everything has a purpose, even suffering and pain.

Love has an enormous purpose in life, better than any purpose on Earth.

Only love has a chance to be everlasting. Only love has eternity.

Only love could prevail over death.

Only love could be strong enough to tolerate pain.

Only love transports life from Earth to heaven,

And from heaven to Earth.

Only love has power over death.

Only love gives life to another.

Only love will survive disaster.

Only love can heal all pain.

— Angela Herrick —

"I had suffering because you had it;

I wasn't free, so I suffered with you.

You may not know that suffering

Makes you a part of me now.

When you suffer, please know

It will be my pain, too!"

Love comes with air;

Without suffering, love would have a short journey.

But love combined with pain will turn sweet air into real feeling.

Real love has its own power;

Nothing and no one can replace it.

Real love is suffering and pain.

Temporary love is

Seductive and will disappear from universe forever.

Eternal love is eternal joy.

The blossom of it is happiness; it is heaven on Earth.

Love will heal pain and will bring peace to your heart.

Love will heal all wounds.

Emotions

When love meets her joy, /for what she suffered too long/,

Then sweetness will show her power, her feeling.

Sweetness will be above love,

Gladness will make her statement,

And around all this harmony will come beauty!

Joy, peace, happiness, sweetness, and beauty-

This is the sweet harmony of the universe!

Believe this: for eternity and sweet harmony,

I would suffer to enter into paradise!

In paradise, you will forget all pain and

Never believe that it existed.

The eternity of paradise will bury the past.

The precious future will open her door

To everlasting paradise.

For all eternity and precious paradise,

Love made her pain.

Love is the only reason to live!

CPSIA information can be obtained at www.ICGtesting.com
Printed in the USA
LVOW07*1337260615

444023LV00003B/8/P